RESOURCE CENTRE
WESTERN ISLES LIBRARIES

Readers are requested to take great care of the books while in their possession, and to point out any defects that they may notice in them to the Librarian.
This book is issued for a period of twenty-one days and should be returned on or before the latest date stamped below, but an extension of the period of loan may be granted when desired.

DATE OF RETURN	DATE OF RETURN	DATE OF RETURN
Bayble 4-5		
23/04/01		
3 1 MAR 2017		
3 0 MAR 2019		
3 0 SEP 2019		

YOUNG CITIZEN...

GROWING UP

Kate Brookes

WAYLAND

Other titles in the series
At Home
At School
In the Street

Editor: Sarah Doughty
Photostylist: Gina Brown
Specially commissioned photographs: Angela Hampton and
Martyn Chillmaid.
With thanks to St.Stephen's Middle School, Redditch for their
help with the commissioned photography.

Designer: Simon Borrough
Illustrator: Mike Flanagan

This edition published in 2000 by
Wayland Publishers Ltd
61 Western Road, Hove
East Sussex BN3 1JD

Find Wayland on the Internet at http://www.wayland.co.uk

British Library Cataloguing in Publication Data
Brookes, Kate
    Growing Up. – (Young Citizen)
    1. Maturation (Psychology) - Juvenile Literature 2. Ethics
    Juvenile literature
    I. Title
    155.2'5

ISBN 0 7502 2346 4

Printed and bound by EuroGrafica S.p.A., Italy

CONTENTS

WITHDRAWN

WHEN I'M OLDER ...

Hands up, who can't wait to be older and able to do whatever they want? Chances are that you and your friends daydream or talk about what you'll do and where you'll go when you're older. But sometimes all this exciting growing up business can seem a little frightening – there are so many things to think about and so many choices to make.

"When I'm older I want to share a flat with my best friend. We'll have to get a job to pay for everything, but that'll be more fun than being at school."
Naomi

"Growing up is confusing. My Mum says I'm old enough to make decisions, but she still tells me when it's bedtime and to eat my vegetables. It doesn't seem fair!" **Kerrie**

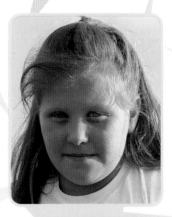

"I can't wait to be a teenager. I'll be able to do whatever I like and my parents won't be able to stop me!"
Gerard

"If growing up means working and cleaning your room and stuff, it doesn't sound like much fun." **Eriko**

"As I get older, I'm changing my mind about lots of things. I can understand why there have to be some rules."
Monica

"Some things about growing up are scary. You've got to pass exams so that you can get a job." **Anya**

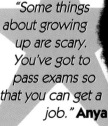

Do you think Gerard has the right idea? Why does Kerrie think growing up is 'confusing'? Monica's ideas are changing. Are yours?

4

Growing up happens slowly, but look at how you change from year to year. Do you feel different to how you felt one or two years ago?

PICK-A-BOX

Can you pick the phrases that describe what 'growing up' means to you? Which are the most important?

Growing up means:

My body changes

Making my own decisions

Going out by myself

Ignoring what my parents say

Having more fun

Staying up really late

Being more helpful

Looking after my things

Cleaning my room

Being more understanding

Being smarter

Bossing little kids about

Getting more pocket money

Having my own TV

I'M JUST TRYING TO BE HELPFUL!

NOBODY UNDERSTANDS!

As you grow older, you're ready to be trusted, responsible and independent. You know you're ready, but others (usually parents) don't. You know you can be trusted to do your homework on time, clean your teeth and feed the goldfish, so why do parents keep nagging? It's because parents are the last to realize that you're growing up, becoming more independent and wanting some control!

Hi, how was school?

OK. I'm going to watch TV.

Any homework tonight?

Heaps!

You don't even know what happens at school. You don't know anything about anything!

Well, hadn't you better do it, then watch TV?

Mum, I know what I have to do and I'll do my homework later.

Mum, I was watching that. You don't control my life.

Maybe not, but you've got to do your school work.

Don't slam that door, Steven!

When is she going to stop bugging me?

Is Steven angry because he can't watch TV or is there another reason?
Should his Mum have turned off the TV?
Did this argument have to happen?
Has something like this ever happened to you?

6

SHUTTING THE DOOR OR SLAMMING

You won't find any solutions to a problem by losing your temper, slamming doors or sulking in your room. They only make things worse. Why? Read on to see what Steven says:

"Storming out and slamming the door were bad moves. My Mum grounded me for a week and banned the TV. I got into a major sulk and tried to get back at her by not doing any homework. No prizes for guessing what happened at school for the non-show of homework. The whole thing was dumb. If I'd kept my cool, I could have worked it so that I watched TV for a little while and then done my homework." **Steven**

GET SMART WITH ADULTS:

1. **Don't lose your cool; stay calm.**
2. **Don't shout; only talking helps.**
3. **Don't be stubborn; find a solution that suits everyone.**
4. **Don't forget to talk about what's really bugging you.**
5. **Be patient; don't forget grown-ups are the last to know that you're growing up!**

THE BIG QUESTION

Why do lots of kids find it easier to talk to their friends than to a parent?

ROLL UP FOR THE ROLLER-COASTER!

As you grow it's easy to see your body changing – sometimes it seems that you grow taller overnight. At the same time, things are happening inside your body that affect the way you behave.

Imagine that your body is a test-tube filled with a mixture of chemicals (and what you had for lunch). As you grow, the chemicals start bubbling. The more they bubble, the more you change. Sometimes they can make you feel great, sometimes they make you feel sad. That's why growing up is like being on a roller-coaster – one minute you're on top of the world, the next you're down in the dumps.

"I don't know what happened, but I was talking to my friends about something on TV, then all of a sudden I was in tears."
Shona

"I was explaining to Dad what happened at school. When he asked me to repeat something, I stormed off saying 'Why don't you listen? Do I have to say everything twice?' I don't know why I lost my temper." **Al**

FACT BOX

Growing from a child into an adult starts some time between the ages of eight and 15. This stage is called puberty and it's when your body starts to change.

And, you know what the really weird thing is – you're usually the last to know that the chemicals are bubbling and your behaviour is changing.

ARE YOU A GOOD TALKER?

Talking is one thing, but how good are you at communicating how you feel? Try this quiz to find out.

1 Your team lost the basketball tournament. When a parent asks how the game went, do you say...
a) Nothing – and run to your room?
b) "What do you care?"
c) "We were thrashed and I'm feeling bad about it."

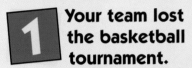 The gang are going to the cinema, and you weren't invited. What do you do?
a) Sulk and feel very sorry for yourself.
b) Pretend to yourself that you don't care what they do.
c) Be honest and admit that you'd like to be with them.

2 The kids at dance class laughed at your dance routine. You feel embarrassed and want to give up. What do you say to the teacher?
a) "I tried really hard with my dance routine. Was it that bad?"
b) "I have to stop dance class, it clashes with bunge jumping."
c) Say nothing and never go again.

3 You feel your parents are being too strict. What do you do?
a) Grumble big-time to your friends.
b) Give your parents the cold-shoulder.
c) Sit down and talk to your parents about how you feel.

SCOREBOARD

1 a) 0 b) 0 c) 2
2 a) 2 b) 0 c) 0
3 a) 0 b) 0 c) 2
4 a) 0 b) 0 c) 2

THE BIG QUESTION

Do you think your parents understand what it's like to be growing up?

WHAT'S YOUR SCORE?

5-8: You're a good communicator because you trust people. You're also honest about your feelings.

Less than 5: You've got to learn to trust people. Getting angry, sulky or closing up like a clam will only make you feel worse. If something is bothering you, go and talk to someone about it.

Under Pressure

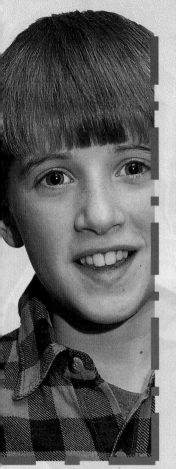

As you get older, you become more aware of everything around you. You notice how others are feeling and how they behave, and how their mood affects you. When everyone is happy, you're happy. But when friends or family are angry or worried, it brings you down.

How would you feel if one of these things happened in your family or to a friend's family?

Winning the Lottery
Losing a job
Going on holiday
Moving house
Getting a puppy
Failing an exam
Dealing with death

IT'S A FACT

If you need help and can't talk to a member of your family, a friend or a teacher, there are counsellors who will talk to you on the phone. Many of these counsellors are specially trained to help young people just like you. You'll find their telephone numbers on page 31.

If sadness or worry last a long time, it can make you depressed and unwell. If you're finding it hard to cope with a problem, don't bottle it up. The best thing to do is ask an adult you trust for help. If you bottle up little problems, they can grow into big ones.

GROWING PAINS

Sometimes growing up and doing new things, moving to a different school and taking on new responsibilities can make you worry. This is what happened to Leena.

Leena Learns

I've got to finish this. Mum's pushing me to do well in the science test.

NEXT MORNING

Leena, you can't go to school without any breakfast.

I can't stop! I'm running late for athletics training. Bye!

Leena, are you OK? You look really pale.

I'm fine. We'd better get to that test.

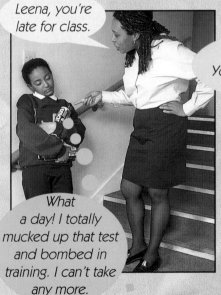

Leena, you're late for class.

What a day! I totally mucked up that test and bombed in training. I can't take any more.

AT HOME

So you flunked the test. You'll have to work much harder.

I can't work any harder. There's too much pressure. What am I going to do?

Is Leena trying to do too much?
What do you think Leena should do?
How could her Mum help her?
Who could Leena talk to?

THE BIG QUESTION

When might it be useful to talk to someone you don't know – such as a counsellor?

11

I CAN'T STAND MYSELF

Here is what some kids think about their bodies:

"I've got a birthmark on my shoulder. The only time I think about it is when I go swimming and it's really noticeable." **Sabrina**

When you were young, you didn't worry about what you looked like. You certainly didn't know the meaning of a 'bad hair day'. Now you're older, you suddenly realize you have a body and that it's different to everyone else's. While brushing your hair, you notice that it is too curly or too straight, too brown or too blond. While changing for swimming, you decide that your legs are too long or too short, too hairy or still totally bare.

Noticing things about your body, the way you look and the way you dress is natural and normal. It's normal not to like some parts of your body.

"My best friend has the most beautiful hair. I used to spent hours trying to make my mop look like hers. What a waste of time and hair gel." **Jo**

"I'd love to be a fashion model and wear beautiful clothes, but I'll never be that thin. Sometimes you can see their bones." **Anita**

"I like all of me except for my freckly face, but the girls at school like my freckles and call me 'Cutie'. So the freckles can stay." **Simon**

"I got a bad scar in an accident. At first, I hid it under shirts and jumpers, but it's a part of me so what's the point of being embarrassed?" **Shaun**

"I've got really skinny legs and my friend has chubby legs. We always joke about swapping legs." **Miguel**

Are these kids happy with the way they look? Do they seem confident and proud? How do you feel about your body and the way you look?

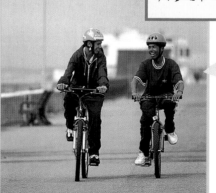

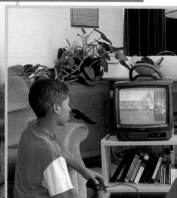

14

To admire someone else's body and how they look is normal. Everyone likes to people-watch. But if someone is always comparing themselves to others and can't find anything good about themselves, it's bad news. They lose their self-esteem and confidence. Some kids feel so bad about themselves that they endanger their health with dieting or do things to hurt their body.

If I looked like that model, my life would be great.

It's not fair. I look like a walking disaster while everyone else has a nice figure.

What is Sharon doing to herself?

Does she have any self-esteem?

Should Sharon talk about how she feels? Would it help her?

Sharon, Mandy wants to know if you want to go swimming?

What? Wear a costume and have them sneer at me. No way!

I hate myself. I hate them. Everything goes wrong for me.

YOUR BODY – THERE'S NO COMPETITION!

Because everyone grows and develops differently and at different times, comparing yourself to others is a waste of time. You are unique and very special in every way and you should be proud of it. If you were Sharon's best friend, what would you say to her?

FACT BOX

Sometimes children make jokes about those who look different. They often find nicknames for the tallest or shortest, the skinniest or fattest, or for those who develop quickly or slowly. If this happens to you, ignore the comments. But if it worries you, talk to someone you trust.

GETTING A LIFE

Being healthy is not just about eating the right stuff and doing exercise. It's about wanting to learn about lots of things, doing new activities and meeting new friends. If you're not out there getting a life, then you're indoors being a couch potato.

Pick the go-getters from the couch potatoes.

"Exercise is so-ooo boring!"

"Why do we need friends when we've got computer games?"

"Why go out? There's nothing to do where I live."

"Can't dance for peanuts, but it's a good laugh."

"Volleyball's great and the team's heaps of fun."

"I'm always starving after a long ride."

THE BIG QUESTION

What can happen if you don't look after your health?

PSST! WANT TO HEAR A SECRET?

Not many people know this, but when you feel happy and healthy, you feel confident. And because you're confident you do more activities. This makes you happier and healthier. On the other hand, the less you do, the sadder and less confident you feel. Eventually, you slide in to couch potatodom.

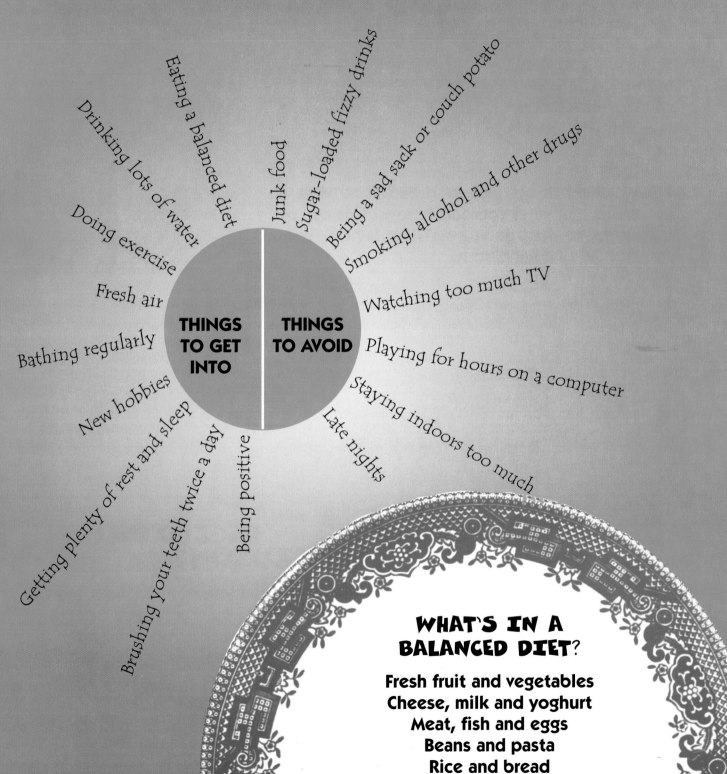

THINGS TO GET INTO
- Eating a balanced diet
- Drinking lots of water
- Doing exercise
- Fresh air
- Bathing regularly
- New hobbies
- Getting plenty of rest and sleep
- Brushing your teeth twice a day
- Being positive

THINGS TO AVOID
- Junk food
- Sugar-loaded fizzy drinks
- Being a sad sack or couch potato
- Smoking, alcohol and other drugs
- Watching too much TV
- Playing for hours on a computer
- Staying indoors too much
- Late nights

WHAT'S IN A BALANCED DIET?

Fresh fruit and vegetables
Cheese, milk and yoghurt
Meat, fish and eggs
Beans and pasta
Rice and bread
Water

EVERYONE SAYS SOMETHING DIFFERENT

When you were younger, your world revolved around your family. Now you're older, your world is bigger. You learn things from school and from friends, from books and magazines, from television and the Internet. Can you think of other ways in which you learn new things?

"Magazines are full of stuff about sex, and when I asked my Mum about something I'd read, she went ballistic and said I'm too young to know about 'these things'. I think she's being old-fashioned. I don't want to upset her, so I'll save my questions for sex education classes at school." **Tobias**

You may hear things that are different to what you believe or what your family says. This can be confusing, so what do you do? This is how Tobias, Jon and Satoshi handled it.

"When my parents were out of doors, I watched a programme that I knew they wouldn't have allowed me to see. It was OK but I've now got a lot of questions that are unanswered. I don't know whether to risk asking and getting into trouble about it." **Jon**

DECISIONS, DECISIONS

As you grow older you want to make more decisions about what you believe in. You and your family or friends may agree on lots of things, sometimes you may disagree. There will also be times when you just can't make up your mind.

"When my best friend told the teacher a fib, I was really sad. It's wrong to tell lies. I'm still thinking about what I'm going to say to my friend." **Satoshi**

MIND READING

1. Some kids in your street play jokes on an elderly person. What do you do?
a) Try to convince them it's a rotten thing to do.
b) Go along with them because they say it's OK.
c) Ignore it, it's none of your business.

2. Your parent says that your best friend in the whole world is a bad influence. What do you do?
a) Decide if he's a good friend, then give your parent a chance to get to know him better.
b) Hang out with him behind your parent's back.
c) Drop your friend because your parent says to.

3. You're not feeling very well, but your mates want you to go swimming. What do you do?
a) Decide if you're well enough, then give them your answer.
b) Ask a parent to come up with an excuse.
c) Go with them because they want you to.

4. The council want to build on the only green playing space near where you live. What do you do?
a) Decide if it's worth saving your play area, ask for more information and see what others in the neighbourhood think.
b) Wait for someone else to do something about it.
c) Nothing, because you don't care?

5. During an RE lesson you hear something that is different to what you and your family believe. What do you do?
a) Talk it over with the teacher and the class, then decide if you should mention it to your parents.
b) Shrug it off – maybe somebody else will sort this one out.
c) Go along with it.

What's your score?
All or mostly **A**s: You can make decisions for yourself and then act on them. Terrific!
All or mostly **B**s: You like sitting on the fence rather than making a decision. Only problem: fence sitting can be uncomfortable and you might fall off!
All or mostly **C**s: You need to exercise your mind; you're not using it at all. Others are doing your thinking for you.

What are the most important things to remember when you're making a decision?
- Honesty
- What your friends will think
- Respect for yourself and others
- Tolerance
- Looking tough
- Fairness
- That you're right and everyone else is wrong.

RIGHT AND WRONG

How do you know if something is right or wrong?
Is is it because...

1 You've been told it is?

2 You've worked it out for yourself?

3 You know it's illegal?

4 You know it could harm you or someone else?

There are some things that everyone believes to be wrong. No one thinks that telling fibs or stealing is right. Can you think of other things that everyone thinks is wrong?

TAKING A WRONG TURN

Why does Jake not want to go with Richard?
Why does the other kid go?
How do you feel about Jake? Would he be a good friend?
Jake wants to stop Richard. What can he do?

Jake knows that driving without a licence is illegal. He has also worked out for himself that it's wrong, because Richard could harm himself or someone else.

18

DOING WHAT'S RIGHT

When you have respect for yourself and for others, doing the right thing comes easy. Why? Having self-respect means that you wouldn't do anything to hurt yourself or wreck your amazing potential. Respecting others means that you'd do nothing to hurt them.

If you respect yourself and others, would you...

shoplift?

joyride?

play hurtful tricks?

bully someone?

take or sell illegal drugs?

call someone horrible names?

bunk off school?

cheat in a test?

IT'S A FACT

Even though the law treats children under the age of 16 differently to adults, children who have broken a law can be punished. They will be questioned by police and have to go to court. A judge in the court may then decide it's best for them to live in a special place, away from their family and friends.

BUT THEY'RE MY FRIENDS

Friends become more and more important as you grow older. You look forward to doing things with them, sharing a laugh and a secret, but you also come to rely on each other. When your friends aren't about, minutes often seem like hours and everything becomes 'boring!'

WHAT MAKES A GOOD FRIENDSHIP?

1. Honesty
This means more than not telling each other fibs, it also means being who you really are (not playing any pretend roles) and saying what you really think (not what your friends want you to say).

"Celina is the best friend you could ever have. When I started hanging around with a bad bunch, she told me she was worried. I told her to mind her own business, but she didn't give up. In the end, I realized she was right." **Rebecca**

2. Trust
Being able to rely on each other through thick and thin. Good friends don't turn their back on you.

"When my Mum and Dad were divorcing, I was a real pain. I was rude to my friends, a total slacker at school and a general misery. When the kids in our class started saying I was bad news, my friend Grieg stood up for me. I'll never forget that." **Jayne**

3. Caring
This is more than just 'liking' your friends. Caring about them means that you would go out of your way to help them.

"I was really sick for ages and I couldn't go to school. I thought my friends would forget me, but they didn't. Chloe came on her bike to see me each day after school. It was good to catch up on the chat. The only problem was she brought my homework, too." **Craig**

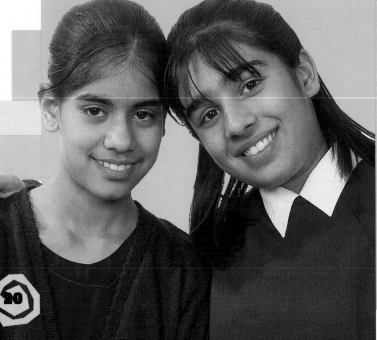

FAKE FRIENDS

Everyone has come across 'fake friends'. These are the ones who pretend to be 'good friends', but are the first to talk about you behind your back, drop you when someone 'better' comes along, and give you the cold-shoulder when you're in trouble. Getting rid of fake friends is usually easy – they generally leave you!

SASHA'S STORY

"I was really flattered when they asked me to join their crowd. The only thing they said was that I'd have to get some smarter clothes if I was going to hang around with them. When I wore my new gear, they laughed and said that they would help me get some better stuff. But they didn't mean buy, they meant steal! I went along with them because I wanted to stay friends. It was the biggest mistake ever. When I got caught shoplifting, they ran off. And you know what they did – they told everyone at school I was a thief and a bad influence. Just one week with them and I became a pathetic wimp with no self-respect. Now, I'm back with a good crowd again who like the 'real' me and my self-respect has returned." **Sasha**

BAD FRIENDS – BAD NEWS

It's harder though to be free of 'bad-news' friends. These are the ones who want you to do what they do, say what they say and think what they think. It's these bods who can get you in trouble. Sasha tells what happened when she fell in with bad friends.

How you can spot bad friends:

1. They often stick to each other like glue and don't have other friends.

2. They start to look and act like clones of each other.

3. They stand up for the group, not for the people in it.

4. They won't let you be yourself. You lose your own identity and self-respect.

If you remember that good friends are honest, trusting and caring, then you'll never fall in with bad friends.

THE BOY/GIRL THING

When you were younger, you would play with children of either sex. But now that you're older, things have changed. Girls and boys seem to be interested in different things and want to play different games. Girls prefer to hang around with other girls and the boys stick together. Sometimes these groups mix, sometimes they tease each other. Sometimes it's as though girls and boys come from different planets and have nothing in common.

Natasha, Frankie and their friends wrote down their ideas about the 'boy/girl thing'.

"My best friends are all girls, but I have lots of friends who are boys. There are some things I wouldn't share with a boy." **Natasha**

"All the boys in our class are silly. They punch each other, play stupid tricks and are always mucking about." **Frankie**

"I love football and I'll join in any game. Some of my girl friends think I'm a bit of a tomboy." **Cassandra**

"At school I hang around with the boys. At home though, my best friend is a girl. We've been friends since we were really little. If my mates see me with Cathy, they start making kissing noises." **Archie**

GIRLS ARE FROM SATURN, BOYS ARE FROM JUPITER

SEE, I TOLD YOU GIRLS WERE ALIENS!

BOOKS

"My twin sister and I are identical – we like the same sort of things and get along really well when we're alone together. But when we're with our friends, we act as though we hate each other. Stupid or what?" **Jez**

"The girls think that they are smarter than boys. Whenever we talk to them, they just roll their eyes and turn away. It's so annoying." Tom

ARE BOYS AND GIRLS DIFFERENT?

It doesn't take a genius to know that girls' and boys' bodies are very different. But do you think boys and girls are different in other ways? This is a difficult question that people have been trying to answer for hundreds of years.

Think about these kids' comments and see if they help you come up with an answer to the questions that follow.

"Which one looks better?" **Jeremy**

"Mum and Dad design houses, but I'd like to actually build them." **Sasha**

"I want to be a nurse. I'd like to look after sick babies." **Rashid**

"I need pocket money too!" **Jasmine**

"That film was so-ooo sad." **Rob**

1. Do boys and girls have different goals and ambitions?
2. Are they given different toys to play with and taught different games?
3. Are boys and girls interested in how they dress and how they look?
4. Do boys and girls feel happy and sad about the same sort of things?
5. Do you think that there are some tasks that only boys should be able to do, and others that only girls should be able to do?

IT'S A FACT

When it's made difficult or impossible for a person to do something because of their sex, it's called sexual discrimination. Sexual discrimination is illegal.

FIRST LOVE

Having a friend who you like more than anyone else is very special. You may like him or her because they make you laugh, because of their kindness or because you've got lots in common. These first special friendships can last a little while or may go on for years.

Here's what some kids think about love and friendship.

"I really like Christopher. He's so funny. We're in the choir and drama club, and he doesn't spend every lunchtime playing football. I might ask him to my birthday party." **Brooke**

"Dom really fancies Sarah. He pretends he doesn't by calling her funny names. I think he's frightened that his mates will tease him." **Kate**

"Jade has always been special. Our parents are good friends and we go running together. I think she likes me as well. We can talk for hours about nothing." **Ben**

"All the girls drool over Max – it's revolting. Max loves all the attention, but he doesn't talk to them. I don't know how they can like someone they don't really know." **Yas**

Which of these are needed to make a special relationship? Are they the same things that are needed to make a good friendship?

Lots of money   Respect   Trust
Kindness   Good looks
Honesty   Being clever
Smart clothes   Generosity
Liking the same things

24

Making special friendships and having good friends does not happen overnight. You have to get to know each other (the good and the bad) and then you earn each other's trust and respect. But telling fibs or making up stories to win a friend doesn't work. Honesty is very important.

Gerald's mistake

Anna will just have to find someone else.

Anna, do you want to do the science project with me?

Gerald, do you want to do the project with me?

Yeah. That'll be great.

Wow, would I ever!

Sure, we can start at lunchtime.

Everyone says you're doing the project with Greta, but you asked me first.

Did you Gerald?

Yes, but I really wanted to do it with you Greta.

Well, I'm not interested in people who dump their friends.

What did Gerald do? Was he being honest? Do you think he'll ever be friends with Anna and Greta again?

Do you want to do the project with me, Anna?

Sure. Maybe Gerald can be the guinea pig?

THE BIG QUESTION

Have you ever treated a friend like this? Did they ever trust you again?

DO I HAVE TO?

You get to do lots of new things as you get older. This is because you've shown you can do them, and that you're becoming responsible and trustworthy.

But because you're now so responsible and trustworthy, it means that you can do more for yourself and for others. You can help around the house, do chores and keep your room tidy.

Growing up isn't just about 'getting more', it's also about 'giving more'. Here are some of your rights matched with your responsibilities. Do you agree with them?

RIGHTS

Going out with friends
Decorating your bedroom
Choosing your own clothes
Making your own snacks
Having a sound system
Having pocket money
Having a pet
Having a party

RESPONSIBILITIES

Coming home at the right time
Keeping your room tidy
Looking after your clothes
Tidying the kitchen when you've finished
Turning it down when asked
Keeping it safe
Caring for it and feeding it
Helping to organize it and clean up afterwards

Have these kids got the right idea about what it means to be growing up and becoming more responsible?

"My parents can't make me do anything now. I don't have to help clear the table after dinner. I'm not a kid any more." **Janine**

"When the teachers ask me to stay behind and help put away the gym equipment, I sneak out the door when they're not looking." **Jack**

"My Mum knows I can look after myself, otherwise she wouldn't let me go out. That's why she's not too worried if I come home late." **Rachel**

"A neighbour pays me to water his garden while he's away. Sometimes I do it, but mostly I water it just before he comes back." **Billy**

I DON'T KNOW WHAT HAPPENED. ALL I SAID WAS THAT I WASN'T GOING TO TIDY MY ROOM, AND BANG – THEY GROUNDED ME!

When a parent or other adult asks you to do something, like putting away dishes or helping in the library, what do you do?

a I do it.

b I moan and say it's not fair.

c I say it's not my turn.

d I come up with an excuse not to do it.

e I do it so badly, they don't ask me again.

f I say I'll do it later and then never do it.

If you answered b, c, d, e or f, are you showing that you're growing up?

I CAN'T TAKE ANYMORE

I CAN'T TAKE ANYMORE

Some children feel that asking for help is a sign that they're not grown-up. But they are so wrong. A sure sign of being mature and responsible is knowing when to ask for help. There are times when asking for help is the only right thing to do.

HELP!

Ted, I don't know what's wrong with you lately. Your work is poor and you don't even seem to care. Is there anything I can do?

No, everything's fine. Can I go now?

Oh no, there's those kids again. Maybe I can sneak past without being seen.

Where do you think you're going? I want to talk to you.

Why don't you just leave me alone? What I have done to you?

Ted, you've been acting really weird. Are you mad with me about something?

No. Why can't everyone just leave me alone?

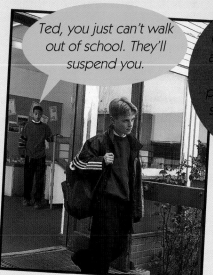

Ted, you just can't walk out of school. They'll suspend you.

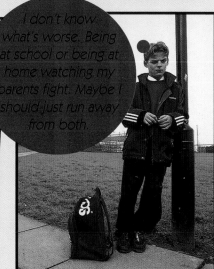

I don't know what's worse. Being at school or being at home watching my parents fight. Maybe I should just run away from both.

What's happened in this story?

Why is Ted having trouble at school?

Will running away solve anything?

Why doesn't he ask for help?

Who could help Ted?

28

GOOD STUFF TO REMEMBER

1 Growing up doesn't mean that you have to cope with everything alone.
2 You're not to blame if there are problems at home.
3 Never be silent if you are being bullied; you're only becoming the victim the bullies want you to be.
4 Don't be embarrassed to show your feelings. Toughing it out won't solve anything.
5 If there are problems at home, find someone you can talk to openly and honestly. It could be a teacher, a school counsellor, a religious leader, a relative, a friend or a friend's parent.
6 Don't let a problem grow so that it overtakes your life.

"I used to love going to Scouts, but these new kids joined and they ruined it for me. When we went camping, they filled my backpack with water and knocked over my stove so that my tent almost caught fire. Even though they did lots of mean things, I stayed really cool. But then one day I went ballistic. The Scout master threw me out of the troop. If I had said something earlier, I'd be in the Scouts and they'd be out." **Stefan**

"When my sister died, I hid how upset I was. I thought my crying would make things harder for Mum and Dad. I was trying to be really strong, helping to run the house and doing chores and stuff. Months later, I fell to pieces and had to go into hospital."
Shareema

"I got into trouble at school and had to give my Mum a note so that she would come and see my teacher. I threw the note away. I knew this was wrong, but I was embarrassed to tell anyone, even my Mum." **Elaine**

THE BIG QUESTION

What's the grown-up thing to do – suffer in silence or call for help?

29

Glossary

Bullying Teasing, frightening, threatening or hurting someone. Often done by a gang or group of kids who pick on one person.

Communicating Being able to express your feelings, ideas and needs to others so that they understand you.

Counsellor A person who can help you sort through a problem or can recommend the best person to help you.

Depressed When you feel sad, pathetic, tired, down-in-the-dumps, and don't know why. Short bouts of sadness occur during puberty and are quite natural. If depression lasts for a long time and is affecting your life, you may need help.

Discrimination Treating someone differently to everyone else because of what they look like, what they wear, what they do, what age they are, where they live or what they believe.

Identity The physical, mental and emotional things that make you yourself. Everyone has their own identity.

Independent Being able to do things for yourself and to have your own thoughts and ideas.

Maturity There are physical changes that makes your body develop, and mark the change from child to adult. Acting in a 'mature way' is when you behave, make decisions and have ideas that are grown-up.

Pride The best side of pride is being confident about who you are and what you can do.

Puberty The period in which your body changes into the body of an adult. The changes in your body go hand-in-hand with changes in your feelings.

Responsibilities Being trusted to do something or to behave in a certain way that does not harm anyone, including yourself.

Rights Those things that everyone should be able to enjoy and share in. You have a right to food, housing, care and protection. As you get older, you and your family will agree on your personal rights. This may include where you can go, what time you come home, having friends around and privacy.

Tolerance Letting others have different beliefs and ways of living.

Trust Being able to rely on someone and to believe them.

Self-respect Believing in yourself and your ideas and treating yourself well.

Books to read

Children Just Like Me by Barnabas and Anabel Kindersley (Dorling Kindersley, 1997)
I Must Tell You Something by Arno Bo (Bloomsbury, 1998)
Stand Up For Your Rights, written by children around the world to mark the 50th anniversary of the Declaration of Human Rights (Two-Can, 1999)
Stories To Make You Think by Heather Butler (Barnabas, 1999)
Understanding Your Body by Rebecca Treays (Usborne, 1998)

Specially for older readers:
Is This Love? and *Wise Guides* – Drugs by Anita Naik (Hodder, 1997/8)
Stand Up For Yourself by Helen Benedict (Hodder, 1997)
Understanding The Facts Of Life by Susan Meredith and Robyn Gee (Usborne, 1998)

Help and advice

If you have problems at home or at school, with your family or with friends, or just need to share your worries, talk to an adult you trust. It could be a family member or relative, a friend's parent, school nurse or counsellor, your doctor, or someone in your religious faith. If you would like to talk to someone who does not know you or your family, call Childline (UK) on 0800 1111. Their telephone service is open 24-hours-a-day, the call is free and won't be listed on a telephone bill.

You can also call the National Society for the Prevention of Cruelty to Children or its Scottish equivalent on 0800 800 5000. Call 1800 666 666 for the Irish Society for the Prevention of Cruelty to Children.

The Samaritans offer a similar service to Childline, though they take calls from people of all ages. The Samaritans can be contacted on 0345 909090.

Careline offers a telephone counselling service for children, young adults and adults. Their number is 0208 514 1177.

For advice on health matters, you should first try to speak to a parent or relative. If that is not possible, a school nurse or counsellor, or your doctor will be able to help.

For information about smoking, alcohol or other drugs call the National Drugs Helpline on 0800 776600. This helpline is free and confidential.

For brochures about keeping safe wherever you are, contact Kidscape at 152 Buckingham Palace Road, London SW1W 9TR or call 0207 730 3300.

Index

Picture acknowledgements

All pictures are from the Wayland Picture Library except p.8 (bottom) Tony Stone Worldwide
(Dennis Kitchen).